Bond

Maths
Assessment Papers

5–6 years

Len and Anne Frobisher

OXFORD
UNIVERSITY PRESS

Great Clarendon Street, Oxford, OX2 6DP, United Kingdom

Oxford University Press is a department of the University of Oxford.
It furthers the University's objective of excellence in research, scholarship,
and education by publishing worldwide. Oxford is a registered trade mark of
Oxford University Press in the UK and in certain other countries

First published by Nelson Thornes Ltd in 2007

British Library Cataloguing in Publication Data
Data available

978-1-4085-1631-7

10 9 8 7 6 5 4 3 2

Printed in Spain

Acknowledgements

Illustrations: Nigel Kitching
Page make-up: Tech-Set Ltd

Although we have made every effort to trace and contact all
copyright holders before publication this has not been possible in all
cases. If notified, the publisher will rectify any errors or omissions at
the earliest opportunity.

Before you get started

What is Bond?

This book is part of the Bond Assessment Papers series for maths, which provides **thorough and continuous practice of all the key maths content** from ages five to thirteen. Bond's maths resources are ideal preparation for many different kinds of tests and exams – from SATs to 11+ and other secondary school selection exams.

What does this book cover?

It covers all the maths that a child of this age would be expected to learn and is fully in line with the National Curriculum for maths and the National Numeracy Strategy. One of the key features of Bond Assessment Papers is that each one practises **a wide variety of skills and question types** so that children are always challenged to think – and don't get bored repeating the same question type again and again. We think that variety is the key to effective learning. It helps children 'think on their feet' and cope with the unexpected.

The age given on the cover is for guidance only. As the papers are designed to be reasonably challenging for the age group, any one child may naturally find him or herself working above or below the stated age. The important thing is that children are always encouraged by their performance. Working at the right level is the key to this.

What does the book contain?

- **20 papers** – each one contains 15 questions.
- **Scoring devices** – there are score boxes in the margins and a progress chart at the back. The chart is a visual and motivating way for children to see how they are doing. Encouraging them to colour in the chart as they go along and to try to beat their last score can be highly effective!
- **Next Steps** – advice on what to do after finishing the papers can be found on the inside back cover.
- **Answers** – located in an easily-removed central pull-out section.
- **Key maths words** – on page 1 you will find a glossary of special key words that are used in the papers. These are highlighted in bold each time that they appear. These words are now used in the maths curriculum and children are expected to know them at this age.

How can you use this book?

One of the great strengths of Bond Assessment Papers is their flexibility. They can be used at home, school and by tutors to:

- provide regular maths practice in **bite-sized chunks**
- **highlight strengths and weaknesses** in the core skills

- identify **individual needs**
- set **homework**
- set **timed formal practice** tests – allow about 25 minutes.

It is best to start at the beginning and work though the papers in order.

What does a score mean and how can it be improved?

If children colour in the progress chart at the back, this will give an idea of how they are doing. The Next Steps inside the back cover will help you to decide what to do next to help a child progress. We suggest that it is always valuable to go over any incorrect answers with children.

Don't forget the website…!

Visit www.bond11plus.co.uk for lots of advice, information and suggestions on everything to do with Bond, exams, and helping children to do their best.

Key words

Some special maths words are used in this book. You will find them in **bold** each time they appear in the papers. These words are explained here.

amount	a collection of objects or money
altogether	usually the total of a set of numbers or the number of objects
calculation	working with numbers to find an answer
count on/ count back	direction of counting on a number line or grid
difference	how many more or less one number is than another number
double	the answer when a number is multiplied by 2
equal	quantities are equal when they have the same number of objects
estimate	a sensible 'guess' at the position of a number on a number line or the quantity of objects in a set
even numbers	whole numbers that can be divided exactly by 2: 2, 4, 6, 8 are even numbers
exact	an answer is exact when it is accurate
face	the surface of a 3D shape
figures	another name for numbers: e.g. 9 rather than 'nine'
less than	a number is less than another number when it is smaller
match	connecting objects, words or numbers which are alike in some way
missing numbers	numbers that are omitted from a sequence or a calculation often represented with a box
more than	a number is more than another number when it is larger
odd numbers	whole numbers that cannot be divided exactly by 2: 1, 3, 5, 7, 9 are odd numbers
order	arranging numbers or objects from smallest to largest or vice versa
pair	a set of 2 objects, shapes or numbers
set	a collection of numbers, shapes or quantities
tens	a digit that represents a whole number of sets of 10
total	the final amount when everything is collected together: the total of 4 and 2 is 6
units	a number between 0 and 9 that represents a single unit at the end of the number: 3<u>4</u> or 13<u>4</u>

Paper 1

1 How many mice?

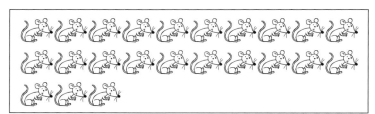

☐

2 Write in the next number.

3–4 **Match** each number to its name.

5 Ring the tallest.

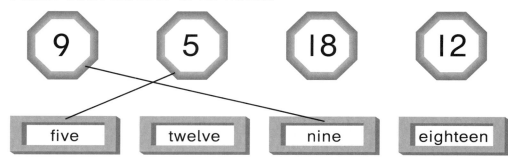

6–7 **Count on** 1. Write in the numbers.

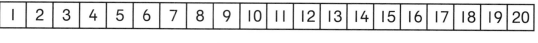

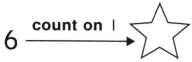

2

8 Guess how many cars.   Ring your guess.

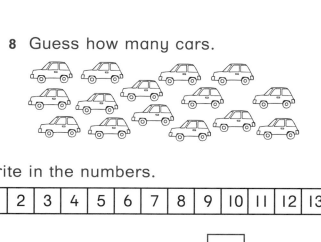

| 5 | 10 | 15 | 20 | 25 |

Write in the numbers.

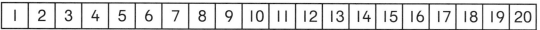

| 1 | 2 | 3 | 4 | 5 | 6 | 7 | 8 | 9 | 10 | 11 | 12 | 13 | 14 | 15 | 16 | 17 | 18 | 19 | 20 |

9 1 **more than** 3 is ☐

10 1 **more than** 17 is ☐

Count on in 10s. Write the next number.

11

10 → 20 → 30 → 40 → ◯

12

40 → 50 → 60 → 70 → ◇

13 How many ducks?

☐

14–15 Count on 2. Write in the number.

| 1 | 2 | 3 | 4 | 5 | 6 | 7 | 8 | 9 | 10 | 11 | 12 | 13 | 14 | 15 | 16 | 17 | 18 | 19 | 20 |

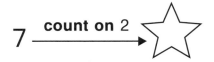

7 —**count on** 2→ ☆   16 —**count on** 3→ ☆

Now go to the Progress Chart to record your score!   Total ◯ 15

3

Paper 2

Write in the answers.

1 3 + 1 = ☐

2 4 + 2 = ☐

3 1 + 5 = ☐

3

4 How many crayons long is the toy plane?

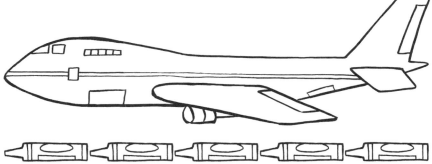

1

5 Colour the number that is less.

21   12

1

6 Colour the number that is more.

41   14

1

7 Ring the coin that is worth the most.

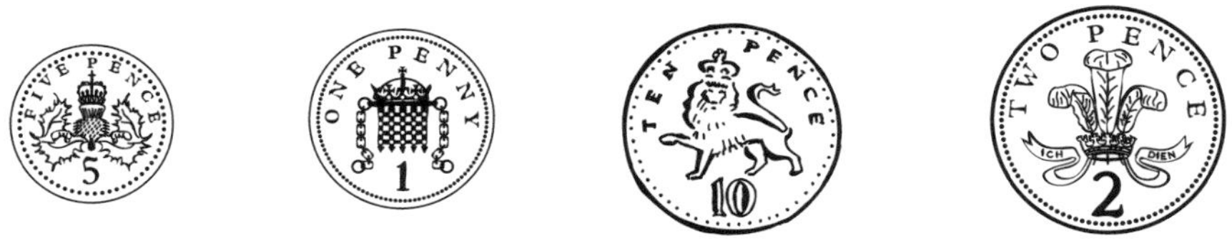

1

8 How many **units** in 17? 1

9 How many **tens** in 14? 1

10–13 **Match** each shape to its name.
One has been done.

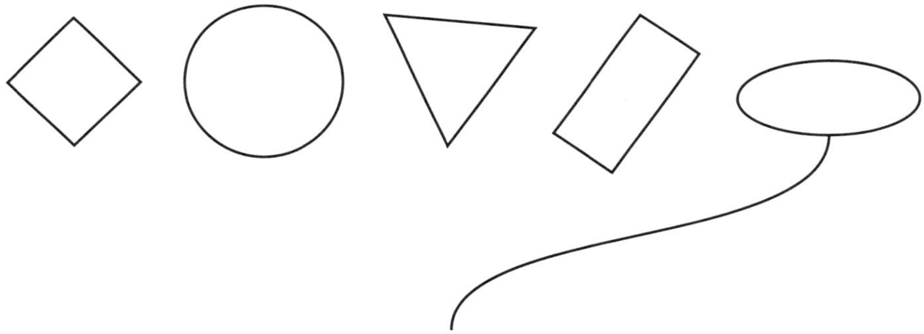

triangle   square   oval   circle   rectangle

4

Write in the answers.

14 What is **double** 1?

15 What is **double** 4?

2

Now go to the Progress Chart to record your score! Total 15

Paper 3

Write in the answers.

1 4 + 1 = ☐

2 3 + 3 = ☐

1	2	3	4	5	6	7	8	9	10

3 5 + 2 = ☐

3

4–7 **Match** each coin to its value.
One has been done.

    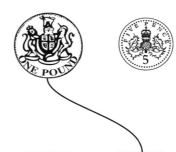

£2	5p	50p	2p	£1

4

Count back. Write in the answers.

1	2	3	4	5	6	7	8	9	10
11	12	13	14	15	16	17	18	19	20

8 What is 7 **count back** 1? ☐

I

9 What is 13 **count back** 1? ☐

I

Write in the answers.

10 5 − 2 = ☐

11 8 − 3 = ☐

| 0 | 1 | 2 | 3 | 4 | 5 | 6 | 7 | 8 |

2

12 Colour the day that comes after Sunday.

| Tuesday | Friday | Monday |
| Saturday | Thursday | Wednesday |

1

13 Colour the day that comes before Sunday.

| Tuesday | Friday | Monday |
| Saturday | Thursday | Wednesday |

1

Write in the **missing numbers**.

14 **Double** 7 is equal to 7 + ☐

15 9 + 9 is equal to **double** ☐

2

Now go to the Progress Chart to record your score!   Total   15

7

Paper 4

Count back in 10s. Write the next numbers.

1

2

3 How much money is in the purse?

☐ p

4 Colour the season that comes before Summer.

| Winter | Spring | Autumn |

5 Colour the season that comes before Autumn.

Winter   Summer   Spring

6 How many sides does this shape have?

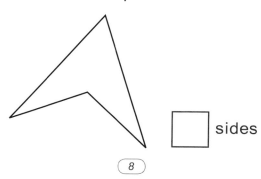

☐ sides

Write in the answers.

7 3 + 2 = ☐

8 5 + 6 = ☐

2

Write in the answer.

9 I **less than** 12 is ☐

1	2	3	4	5	6	7	8	9	10
11	12	13	14	15	16	17	18	19	20
21	22	23	24	25	26	27	28	29	30
31	32	33	34	35	36	37	38	39	40

10 I **less than** 27 is ☐

2

11 Colour the season that comes after Spring.

Winter	Summer	Autumn

1

12 Colour the season that comes after Winter.

(Summer)   (Spring)   (Autumn)

1

13–14 Write in the **missing number** and number name.

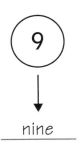
nine

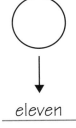
eleven

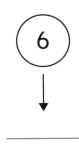
_____

three

2

15 Start at 7. **Count on** 2 tens. Colour the number you get to.

1	2	3	4	5	6	7	8	9	10
11	12	13	14	15	16	17	18	19	20
21	22	23	24	25	26	27	28	29	30

1

Paper 5

1　Shahid's pad is 4 paperclips high.

　Guess how many paperclips wide it is.

2　Tick (✓) the coins needed to make 12p.

Write in the answers.

1	2	3	4	5	6	7	8	9	10

3　$7 - 5 =$ ☐　　　4　$9 - 4 =$ ☐

Count on in 1s.

Write the next numbers.

5　33 → 34 → 35 → 36 → ◯

6　86 → 87 → 88 → 89 → ◇

10

7 Write the **missing number** name.

first   second   _____

⬤ **1**

8 There are 10 cars in each box.
How many cars are there **altogether** in the three boxes?

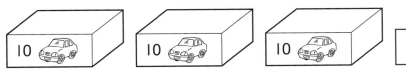

⬤ **1**

9 Write the numbers
from the oval in **order**,
smallest first.

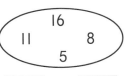

⬛ ⬛ ⬛ ⬛

⬤ **1**

Write in the answers.

1	2	3	4	5	6	7	8	9	10

10 $8 - 2 =$ ⬛   **11** $8 - 6 =$ ⬛

⬤ **2**

12 Ring the heavier parcel.

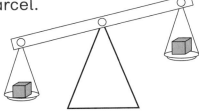

⬤ **1**

Write in the **missing numbers**.

13 $4 + 2 = 2 +$ ⬛   **14** $1 + 3 =$ ⬛ $+ 1$

15 ⬛ $+ 3 = 3 + 2$

⬤ **3**

Paper 6

1 Tick (✓) the coins needed to pay the **exact** price of the orange.

    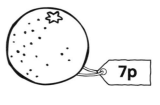

Write in the answers.

2 **Double** 2 = ☐

3 **Double** 5 = ☐

4 How many bricks does the toy bear weigh?

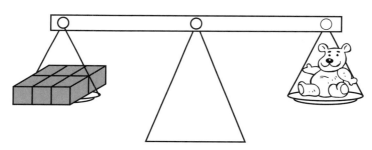

☐

5 Colour the month that comes between April and June.

(January) (March) (May) (July) (September)

6 Colour the number between 24 and 26.

| 21 | 22 | 23 | 24 | 25 | 26 | 27 | 28 | 29 | 30 |

7 Colour the number between 31 and 33.

| 31 | 32 | 33 | 34 | 35 | 36 | 37 | 38 | 39 | 40 |

Write in the next **calculation** in the patterns.

8 10 + 1 = 11   9 10 − 1 = 9
   10 + 2 = 12   10 − 2 = 8
   10 + 3 = 13   10 − 3 = 7

   | 10 | + | | = | | | 10 | − | | = | |

○ 2

10 Write 26 in words. _____

○ 1

11 Write thirty-four in **figures**. | |

○ 1

12 Start at 53 in the number grid.
    Count back 2 tens.
    Colour the number you get to.

1	2	3	4	5	6	7	8	9	10
11	12	13	14	15	16	17	18	19	20
21	22	23	24	25	26	27	28	29	30
31	32	33	34	35	36	37	38	39	40
41	42	43	44	45	46	47	48	49	50
51	52	53	54	55	56	57	58	59	60

○ 1

Write in the answers.

13 4 + 3 = | | 14 2 + 5 = | |

○ 2

15 Work out the **missing number**.

(15) —— **count on** 5 tens ——▶ | |

○ 1

1 What is the **total** value of the coins in the bag?

☐ p

Write in the answers.

1	2	3	4	5	6	7	8	9	10	11	12	13	14	15	16	17	18	19	20

2 $14 - 2 =$ ☐   3 $17 - 6 =$ ☐

4–5 Look at the picture.

Colour the correct word in each sentence.

The lamp is to the ⟨left⟩ ⟨right⟩ of the television.

The television is ⟨on top of⟩ ⟨below⟩ the table.

○ 1

○ 2

○ 2

Write in the answers.

6 I **more than** 8 is ☐

7 10 **more than** 11 is ☐ 2

8 How many corners does this shape have?

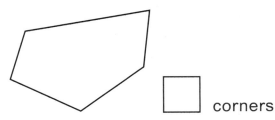

☐ corners 1

Write in the answers.

9 (96) **count back** 5 → ☐   **10** (72) **count back** 20 → ☐ 2

11–13 Write the time the clocks show.

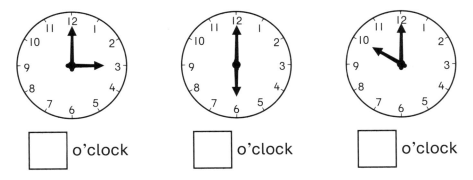

☐ o'clock   ☐ o'clock   ☐ o'clock 3

Write in the answers.

| 0 | 10 | 20 | 30 | 40 | 50 | 60 | 70 | 80 | 90 | 100 |

14 What is 30 add 20? ☐

15 What is 70 add 10? ☐ 2

Paper 8

1 How many cows? ☐ cows

Write in the answers.

2 1 **more than** 19 is ☐

3 1 **more than** 57 is ☐

4 1 **more than** 99 is ☐

5 Ring the coin that is worth the least.

Write in the answers.

6 **Double** 3 = ☐   7 **Double** 6 = ☐

8 Tick (✓) the coins needed to make 24p.

Write in the answers.

9 1 **less than** 6 is ☐

10 10 **less than** 16 is ☐

11–13 Ring the name of each shape.

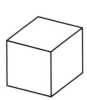  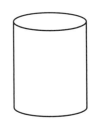

cone	cone	cone
cylinder	cylinder	cylinder
cube	cube	cube
sphere	sphere	sphere

Write in the answers.

14 13 − 3 = ☐

15 19 − 5 = ☐

Now go to the Progress Chart to record your score! Total ◯ 15

17

Paper 9

1 Tick (✓) the coins needed to pay the **exact** price of the cake.

     15p

2 Colour the month that is between October and December.

March   May   July

September   November

Count back in 1s. Write in the next numbers.

3 47 ⟶ 46 ⟶ 45 ⟶ 44 ⟶ ☐

4 73 ⟶ 72 ⟶ 71 ⟶ 70 ⟶ ☐

5 Write in the **missing number**.

5th _____   _____   3rd   2nd   1st

6 Write 51 in words. _____

7 Write sixty-eight in **figures**. ☐

8 Sam has counters in each hand.

left hand   right hand

Complete the table.

Hand	Number of counters
left	5
right	

9 Write in the answer.

 count back 4 tens ⟶ ▢

Write in the answers.

| 1 | 2 | 3 | 4 | 5 | 6 | 7 | 8 | 9 | 10 | 11 | 12 | 13 | 14 | 15 | 16 | 17 | 18 | 19 | 20 |

10 Add 7 to 9. ▢   **11** Add 3 to 16. ▢

Look at the **set** of shapes.

12 How many cubes? ▢

13 How many cones? ▢

14 How many cylinders? ▢

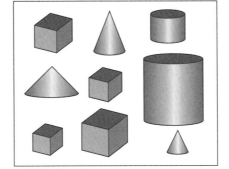

15 What is 17 take away 5? ▢

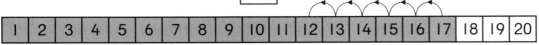

Paper 10

1 How many houses? [   ] houses

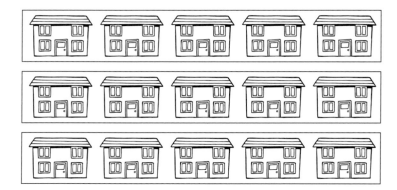

2 How many **units** in 19? [   ]

3 How many **tens** in 13? [   ]

4 How many **units** in 12? [   ]

5 Look at the table.

Name	Number of teddy bears
Alice	2
Sam	6
Sala	3
Chris	5

How many teddy bears does Chris have? [   ]

6 Write a number that is between 60 and 67. [   ]

7 Write a number that is between 79 and 84. [   ]

Paper 1

1 23 **2** 7

3–4

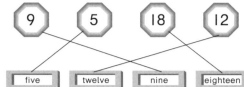

5

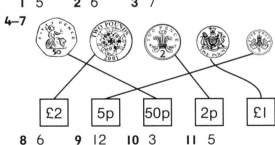

6 7 **7** 14 **8** 15 **9** 4 **10** 18
11 50 **12** 80 **13** 30 **14** 9 **15** 19

Paper 2

1 4 **2** 6 **3** 6 **4** 5 **5** 12
6 41 **7** **8** 7 **9** 1

10–13

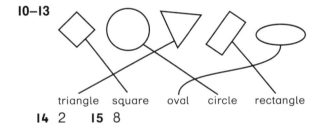

14 2 **15** 8

Paper 3

1 5 **2** 6 **3** 7

4–7

8 6 **9** 12 **10** 3 **11** 5
12 Monday **13** Saturday
14 7 **15** 9

Paper 4

1 10 **2** 50 **3** 4p **4** Spring
5 Summer **6** 4 **7** 5
8 11 **9** 11 **10** 26 **11** Summer
12 Spring **13** 11 **14** six **15** 27

Paper 5

1 3

2

3 2 **4** 5 **5** 37 **6** 90
7 third **8** 30 **9** 5, 8, 11, 16
10 6 **11** 2

12

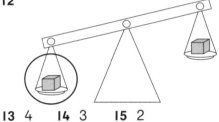

13 4 **14** 3 **15** 2

Paper 6

1

2 4 **3** 10 **4** 6 **5** May
6 25 **7** 32 **8** 10 + 4 = 14
9 10 − 4 = 6 **10** twenty-six
11 34 **12** 33 **13** 7 **14** 7 **15** 65

Paper 7

1 9p **2** 12 **3** 11 **4** left
5 on top of **6** 9 **7** 21
8 5 **9** 91 **10** 52
11 3 o'clock **12** 6 o'clock
13 10 o'clock **14** 50 **15** 80

Bond Maths Assessment Papers 5–6 years

ANSWERS

Paper 8

1 27 2 20 3 58 4 100

5

6 6 7 12

8

9 5 10 6 11 cube
12 cone   13 cylinder
14 10 15 14

Paper 9

1

2 November 3 43 4 69 5 4th
6 fifty-one 7 68 8 4 9 21
10 16 11 19 12 4 13 3 14 2
15 12

Paper 10

1 15 2 9 3 1 4 2 5 5
6 any number from:
  61, 62, 63, 64, 65, 66
7 any number from: 80, 81, 82, 83
8 30 9 8 10 8 11 5 12 4
13 38
14

15

Paper 11

1–2
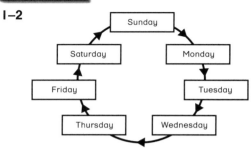

3 9 4 15
5 29 6 43
7 any number from:
  18, 19, 20, 21, 22
8 any number from: 40, 41, 42, 43
9–11

cone pyramid cuboid sphere

12

13 no
14 yes
15 no

Paper 12

1 8 2 1 3 5
4–6
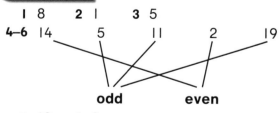

odd   even

7 10 8 9
9 8 10 18
11 20 12 8
13 10 14 30
15 70

A2

Paper 13

1 14   2 42

3

4 10   5 10   6 4   7 3

8 5   9 32   10 6   11 0

12

13 18   14 29   15 38

Paper 14

1 27p   2 13   3 17   4 5   5 51

6 62   7 8   8 36   9 69

10 8:00 OR 8 o'clock

11 3:30 OR Half past 3

12 5   13 8   14 35   15 44

Paper 15

1 6   2 7   3 6   4 39   5 44

6 Davina   7 8, 15, 23   8 6

9 4   10 8   11 22   12 35

13

14 3   15 4

Paper 16

1 25   2 30   3 9   4 9   5 30

6 24   7 45   8 95   9 38   10 47

11 26   12 29   13 10 minutes

14 43   15 47

Paper 17

1 10   2 10

3

4 8

5 16

6 27

7 33

8 £1.21

9 17

10 34

11–13

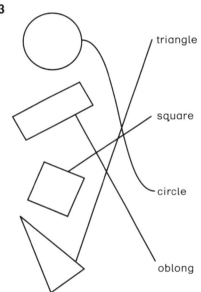

triangle

square

circle

oblong

14 53   15 71

Paper 18

1 11 + 6 = 17

2 11 − 6 = 5

3–5

flat **faces**   curved **faces**

6 31, 23, 21, 13, 12

7 2

8 7

9–11

	odd	even
1	✓	
8		✓
13	✓	
17	✓	
26		✓

12 11:30 OR Half past 11
13 1:00 OR 1 o'clock
14 12   15 25

Paper 19

1

2 2   3 7   4 17   5 9   6 8

7 7 **tens** 3 **units**
8 any numbers from: 29, 30, 31, 32, 33, 34, 35, 36, 37, 38, 39
9 20   10 70   11 66   12 5   13 3
14 25p 15 8p

Paper 20

1 9   2 9

3–5	Number of cubes	Colour of cubes
	5	black (white) grey
	2	(black) white grey
	4	black white (grey)

6 16   7 18   8 10p
9 32   10 53
11 12:30 OR Half past 12
12 6:30 OR Half past 6
13 29   14 27   15 47

8 How many lambs? ☐ lambs

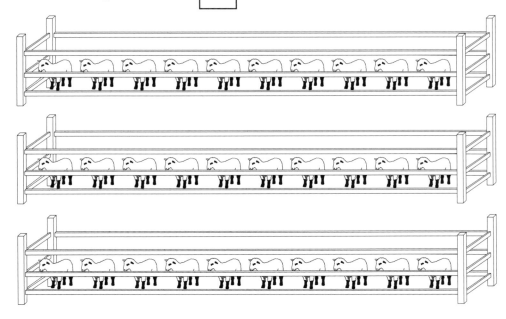

Write in the answers.

9 7 + 1 = ☐

10 5 + 3 = ☐

Write in the **missing numbers**.

11 25 is 2 **tens** and ☐ **units**.

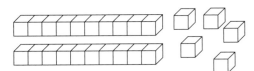

12 41 is ☐ **tens** and 1 **unit**.

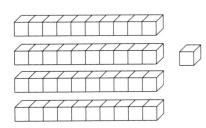

13 3 **tens** and 8 **units** is ☐

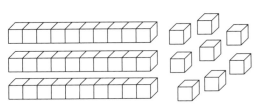

14 Colour the arrow pointing left.

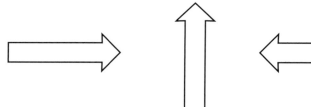

15 Ring the man walking down.

Now go to the Progress Chart to record your score! Total 15

Paper 11

1–2 Write in the missing days.

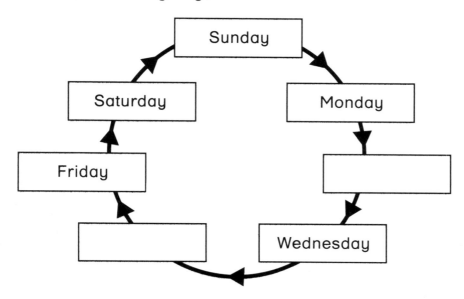

Write in the answers.

3 7 + 2 = ☐

4 11 + 4 = ☐

1	2	3	4	5	6	7	8	9	10
11	12	13	14	15	16	17	18	19	20
21	22	23	24	25	26	27	28	29	30
31	32	33	34	35	36	37	38	39	40
41	42	43	44	45	46	47	48	49	50

5 What number is 10 **more than** 19? ☐

6 What number is 10 **more than** 33? ☐

Write a number that is between each **pair** of numbers.

7 17 ☐ 23

8 39 ☐ 44

9–11 Match each shape to its name.

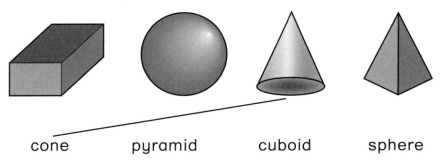

cone   pyramid   cuboid   sphere

12 Ring the jar that holds the most.

This washing machine is off.
For each question below ring
the correct answer.

13–15 Sarah turns it from off to 1.
Has she turned it half a turn?

Yes   No

Asa turns it from off to 2.
Has she turned it half a turn?

Yes   No

Kalid turns it from off to 3.
Has he turned it half a turn?

Yes   No

Now go to the Progress Chart to record your score!   Total   15

24

Paper 12

Write in the answers.

1 9 − 1 = ☐

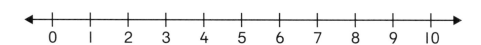

2 9 − 8 = ☐

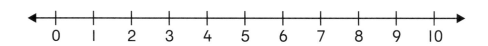

3 9 − 4 = ☐

4–6 Draw lines to **match** each number to the correct answer of **odd** or **even**.

14   5   11   2   19

odd   even

Write in the **missing numbers**.

7 10 + 10 is **equal** to **double** ☐

8 **Double** 9 is **equal** to 9 + ☐

9 Work out the answer.

4  fill

How many fill ? ☐ cups

10–11 **Count on** in 2s. Write in the **missing numbers**.

14 ── **count on 2** ──▶ 16 ── **count on 2** ──▶ ⬠ ── **count on 2** ──▶ ⬠

○ |

○ 2

Write in the answers.

12 4 + 1 + 3 = ☐

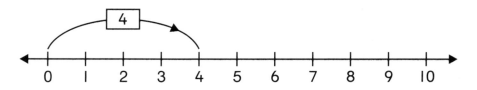

13 3 + 2 + 5 = ☐

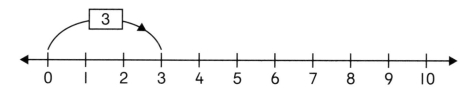

○ 2

Write in the answers.

14 What is 35 − 5? ☐

15 What is 79 − 9? ☐

○ 2

Now go to the Progress Chart to record your score! Total ○ 15

26

Paper 13

Count on.
Write in the numbers.

1

2

3 Tick (✓) the shortest pencil.

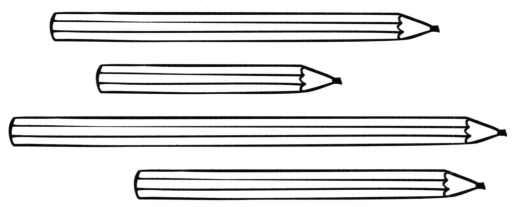

Write in the answers.

4 7 + 3 = ☐   5 4 + 6 = ☐

6–8 How many **equal** sides does each shaded shape have?

☐ **equal** sides   ☐ **equal** sides   ☐ **equal** sides

27

9 Start at 2.
Count on 3 **tens**.
What number did you get to? ☐

1	2	3	4	5	6	7	8	9	10
11	12	13	14	15	16	17	18	19	20
21	22	23	24	25	26	27	28	29	30
31	32	33	34	35	36	37	38	39	40
41	42	43	44	45	46	47	48	49	50

○ **1**

Write in the answers.

10 $7 - 1 = $ ☐   **11** $4 - 4 = $ ☐

○ **2**

12 Adam has this **amount** of money.

Colour the number of 1p coins that make the same **amount** as Adam's money.

○ **1**

13 **Count on** in 3s.
Write in the **missing number**.

0 → 3 → 6 → 9 → 12 → 15 → ⬡

○ **1**

Write in the answers.

14 $24 + 5 = $ ☐

15 $32 + 6 = $ ☐

1	2	3	4	5	6	7	8	9	10
11	12	13	14	15	16	17	18	19	20
21	22	23	24	25	26	27	28	29	30
31	32	33	34	35	36	37	38	39	40
41	42	43	44	45	46	47	48	49	50

○ **2**

Paper 14

1 How much money is in the purse?

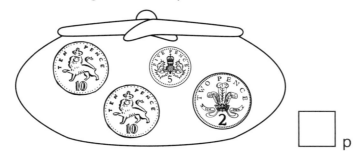

☐ p

Write in the answers.

2 6 + 7 = ☐

3 9 + 8 = ☐

4 Start at 45.
   Count back 4 **tens**.

   What number
   did you get to? ☐

1	2	3	4	5	6	7	8	9	10
11	12	13	14	15	16	17	18	19	20
21	22	23	24	25	26	27	28	29	30
31	32	33	34	35	36	37	38	39	40
41	42	43	44	45	46	47	48	49	50

Write in the answers.

5 (48) **count on** 3 → ☐

6 (12) **count on** 50 → ☐

7 How many squares tall is the bottle?

☐ squares

29

Write in the answers.

8 What number is 10 **less than** 46? ▢

9 What number is 10 **less than** 79? ▢   ◯ 2

10–11 What time do the clocks show?

_____   _____   ◯ 2

Write in the answers.

12 10 − 5 = ▢   13 10 − 2 = ▢   ◯ 2

Write in the answers.

14 28 + 7 = ▢

1	2	3	4	5	6	7	8	9	10
11	12	13	14	15	16	17	18	19	20
21	22	23	24	25	26	27	28	29	30
31	32	33	34	35	36	37	38	39	40
41	42	43	44	45	46	47	48	49	50

15 36 + 8 = ▢   ◯ 2

Paper 15

1–3 How many corners does each shape have?

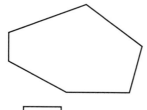 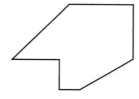 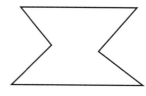

[ ] corners   [ ] corners   [ ] corners

3

4 What number is 1 **less than** 40? [ ]

1

5 What number is 10 **less than** 54? [ ]

1

6 Look at the table. Ring the name of the child who has the most marbles.

Name	Number of marbles
Rick	12
Adam	4
Davina	15
Fran	11

1

7 Write the numbers from the oval in **order**, smallest first.

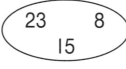

[ ]   [ ]   [ ]
smallest

1

Write in the answers.

8 9 − 3 = [ ]   **9** 9 − 5 = [ ]

2

10 Six 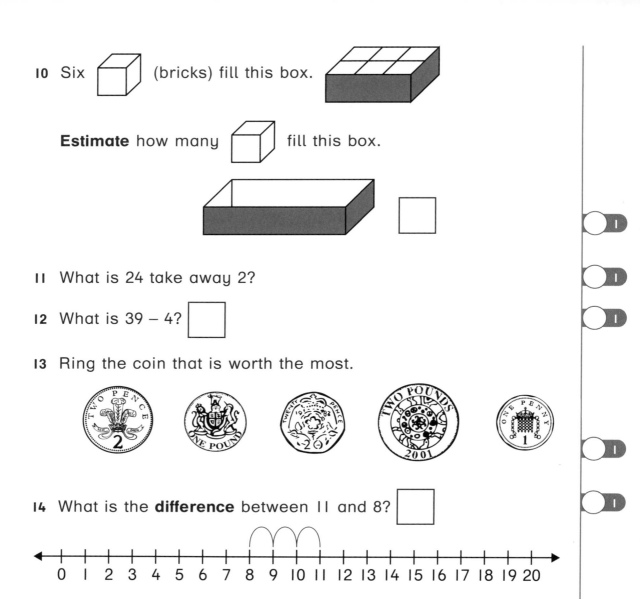 (bricks) fill this box.

Estimate how many fill this box.

11 What is 24 take away 2?

12 What is 39 – 4?

13 Ring the coin that is worth the most.

14 What is the **difference** between 11 and 8?

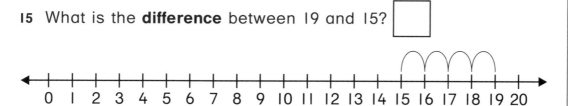

15 What is the **difference** between 19 and 15?

Now go to the Progress Chart to record your score! Total 15

Paper 16

1–2 **Count on** in 5s.
Write in the **missing numbers**.

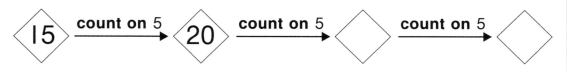

15 — **count on** 5 → 20 — **count on** 5 → ⬦ — **count on** 5 → ⬦

[2]

Write in the answers.

3 6 + 3 = ☐   **4** 1 + 8 = ☐

[2]

5 Rick has 29 toy cars.
Ros has 1 car **more than** Rick.
How many cars does Ros have? ☐

[1]

Write in the answers.

1	2	3	4	5	6	7	8	9	10
11	12	13	14	15	16	17	18	19	20
21	22	23	24	25	26	27	28	29	30
31	32	33	34	35	36	37	38	39	40
41	42	43	44	45	46	47	48	49	50

6 28 − 4 = ☐   **7** 47 − 2 = ☐

[2]

8 Alice has 85 football cards.
Ali has 10 cards **more than** Alice.
How many cards does Ali have? ☐

Beckham

[1]

Write in the answers.

9 31 + 7 = ☐   **10** 43 + 4 = ☐

[2]

Write in the answers.

1	2	3	4	5	6	7	8	9	10
11	12	13	14	15	16	17	18	19	20
21	22	23	24	25	26	27	28	29	30

11 15 + 11 = ☐   12 13 + 16 = ☐

2

13 Aurek lives near school.
Colour the best **estimate** for how long
it takes her to walk to school.

(1 minute)   (10 minutes)

(100 minutes)

1

Write in the answers.

1	2	3	4	5	6	7	8	9	10
11	12	13	14	15	16	17	18	19	20
21	22	23	24	25	26	27	28	29	30
31	32	33	34	35	36	37	38	39	40
41	42	43	44	45	46	47	48	49	50

14 What is 13 add 30? ☐

15 What is 27 add 20? ☐

2

Paper 17

Write in the answers.

1 8 + 2 = ☐   **2** 3 + 7 = ☐   2

3 Tick (✓) the coins needed to pay the **exact** price of the toy fish.

30p

1

Write in the answers.

4 What is **double** 4? ☐   **5** What is **double** 8? ☐   2

Write in the answers.

6 18 + 9 = ☐   **7** 24 + 9 = ☐   2

8 How much money is in the bag?   £ ☐   1

Write in the answers.

9 22 − 5 = ☐

1	2	3	4	5	6	7	8	9	10
11	12	13	14	15	16	17	18	19	20
21	22	23	24	25	26	27	28	29	30
31	32	33	34	35	36	37	38	39	40
41	42	43	44	45	46	47	48	49	50

10 41 − 7 = ☐

○ 2

11–13 **Match** each shape to its name.
One has been done.

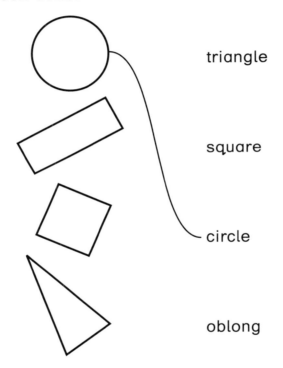

triangle

square

circle

oblong

○ 3

Write in the answers.

14 48 + 5 = ☐   **15** 65 + 6 = ☐

○ 2

Now go to the Progress Chart to record your score!   Total ○ 15

Paper 18

1–2 Write in the next **calculation** in the patterns.

11	+	9	=	20
11	+	8	=	19
11	+	7	=	18

11	−	9	=	2
11	−	8	=	3
11	−	7	=	4

[11] + [ ] = [ ]   [11] − [ ] = [ ]

3–5 **Match** each shape to the type of **face** it has.

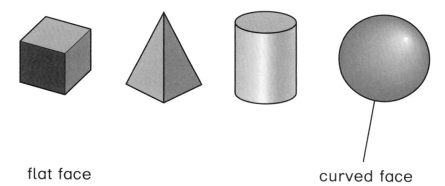

flat face   curved face

6 Write the numbers from the oval in **order**, largest first.

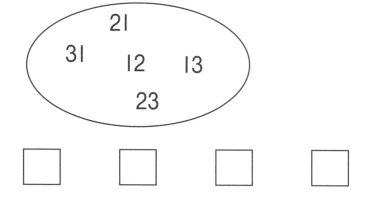

[ ] [ ] [ ] [ ] [ ]

largest

Write in the answers.

7 10 − 8 = [ ]   **8** 10 − 3 = [ ]

37

9–11 Put a tick (✓) in the correct column to show whether the numbers are **odd** or **even**.

	odd	even
1	✓	
8		✓
13		
17		
26		

3

12–13 Write the times the clocks show.

_____   _____

2

Write in the answers.

14 $21 - 9 = \boxed{}$ **15** $34 - 9 = \boxed{}$

2

Paper 19

1   Tick (✓) the coins needed to pay the **exact** price of the tennis ball.

2   9 – 7 = ☐   3   9 – 2 = ☐

4   Some children put a brick for the colour they like best.

Altogether, how many bricks are there? ☐ bricks

Favourite colours

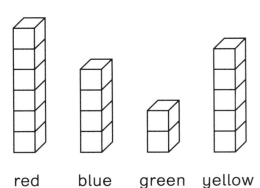

red   blue   green   yellow

Write in the **missing numbers**.

5   29 = 2 **tens** and ☐ **units**

6   84 = ☐ **tens** and 4 **units**

7   73 = ☐ **tens** and ☐ **units**

8 Write a number that is between 28 and 40. ☐

Write in the answers.

1	2	3	4	5	6	7	8	9	10
11	12	13	14	15	16	17	18	19	20
21	22	23	24	25	26	27	28	29	30
31	32	33	34	35	36	37	38	39	40
41	42	43	44	45	46	47	48	49	50
51	52	53	54	55	56	57	58	59	60
61	62	63	64	65	66	67	68	69	70
71	72	73	74	75	76	77	78	79	80
81	82	83	84	85	86	87	88	89	90
91	92	93	94	95	96	97	98	99	100

9 $50 - 30 =$ ☐

10 $90 - 20 =$ ☐

Write in the answers.

11 $57 + 9 =$ ☐

12 What is the **difference** between 32 and 37? ☐

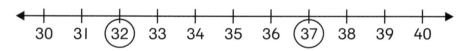

13 What is the **difference** between 48 and 51? ☐

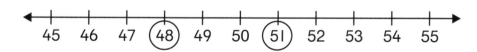

14 Ben has 15p. His grandma gives him 10p.

How much does he have **altogether**? ☐ p

15 Tessa buys a 12p orange. She pays with a 20p coin.

How much change should she get? ☐ p

Paper 20

Write in the answers.

1 5 + 4 = ☐   **2** 2 + 7 = ☐

2

3–5 Sahid has a **set** of black, white and grey cubes.

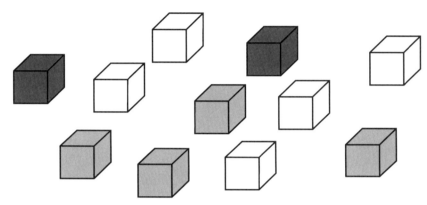

He makes a table.

Ring the correct colour for each number of cubes.

Number of cubes	Colour of cubes
5	black white grey
2	black white grey
4	black white grey

3

Write in the answers.

6 7 + 3 + 6 = ☐

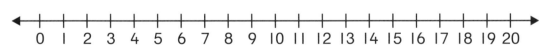

7 8 + 1 + 9 = ☐

2

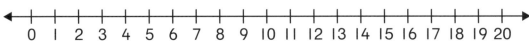

8 Becky buys the apple

with this coin.  10p

How much change does she get? ☐ p

Work out the answers.

9 35 − 3 = ☐

10 59 − 6 = ☐

11–12 Write the time the clocks show.

_____

_____

Write in the answers.

13 17 + 12 = ☐

1	2	3	4	5	6	7	8	9	10
11	12	13	14	15	16	17	18	19	20
21	22	23	24	25	26	27	28	29	30

14 14 + 13 = ☐

1	2	3	4	5	6	7	8	9	10
11	12	13	14	15	16	17	18	19	20
21	22	23	24	25	26	27	28	29	30

Write in the answer.

15 56 − 9 = ☐

1

2

2

2

1

Now go to the Progress Chart to record your score!   Total   15

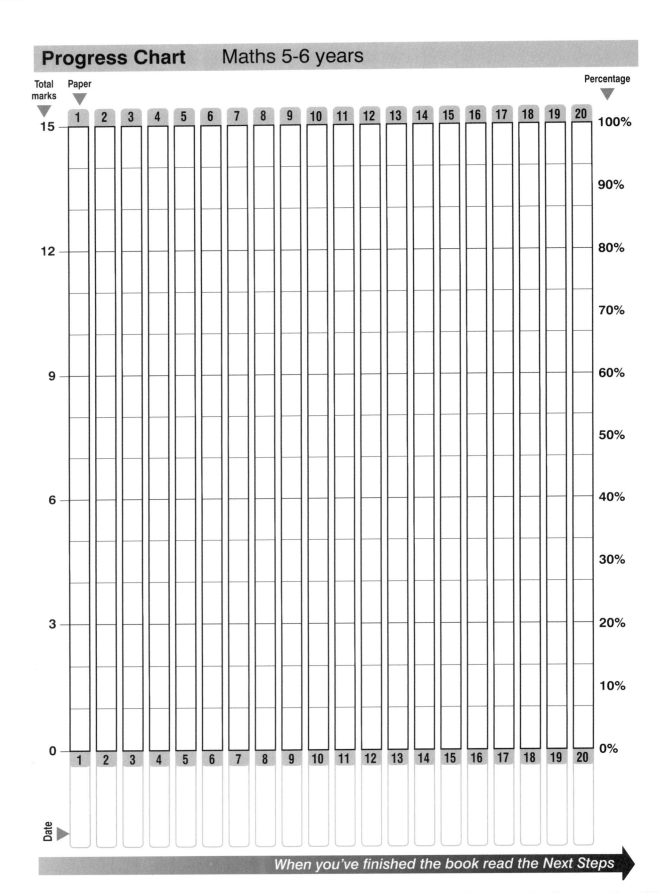

Progress Chart   Maths 5-6 years

Total marks ▼

Paper ▼

Percentage ▼

| | 1 | 2 | 3 | 4 | 5 | 6 | 7 | 8 | 9 | 10 | 11 | 12 | 13 | 14 | 15 | 16 | 17 | 18 | 19 | 20 | |

15 — 100%

90%

12 — 80%

70%

9 — 60%

50%

6 — 40%

30%

3 — 20%

10%

0 — 0%

| 1 | 2 | 3 | 4 | 5 | 6 | 7 | 8 | 9 | 10 | 11 | 12 | 13 | 14 | 15 | 16 | 17 | 18 | 19 | 20 |

Date ▶

When you've finished the book read the Next Steps ➤